100 BOOKS ON ISLAM IN ENGLISH
and
THE END OF ORIENTALISM
in Islamic Studies

OTHER TITLES BY HRH PRINCE GHAZI BIN MUHAMMAD

Love in the Holy Qur'an
What is Islam and Why?

EDITED TITLES

War and Peace in Islam:
The Uses and Abuses of Jihad

100 BOOKS ON ISLAM IN ENGLISH
and
THE END OF ORIENTALISM
in Islamic Studies

HRH Prince Ghazi bin Muhammad

THE ISLAMIC TEXTS SOCIETY

Copyright © The Prince Ghazi Trust for Quranic Thought 2014

This first edition published 2014 by
The Islamic Texts Society
Miller's House
Kings Mill Lane
Great Shelford
Cambridge CB22 5EN, U.K.

British Library Cataloguing-in-Publication Data.
A catalogue record for this book is
available from the British Library.

ISBN 978 1903682 883

The right of Ghazi bin Muhammad to be identified as author
of this work has been asserted by him in accordance with the
Copyright, Designs and Patents Act 1988.

*All rights reserved. No part of this publication may be produced,
installed in retrieval systems, or transmitted in any form
or by any means, electronic, mechanical, photocopying,
recording, or otherwise, without the prior written
permission of the publishers.*

CONTENTS

Part I
The End of Orientalism in Islamic Studies
page 1

Part II
100 Books on Islam in English:
25 Essential & 50 Excellent Books on Islam in English
page 11
25 Recommended Books on Islam in English
page 28

Part III
33 General, Necessary Books and 7 Reference Works
page 33

About the Author
page 39

PART I
THE END OF ORIENTALISM IN ISLAMIC STUDIES

In 1978, the late Arab Christian Professor Edward Said published his famous work *Orientalism*. The book—followed by a smaller volume called *Covering Islam*—suggested a number of interesting things, but one of the main ideas was that the West's distorted view of Islam—in particular in the Western-dominated spheres of academia and the media—has insinuated itself into the Islamic world to such an extent, that Muslims (and/or 'Easterners' in general) had begun to see themselves not as they actually are, or as they have always seen themselves, but rather as the West sees them. In other words, Muslims had come to believe Western caricatures of themselves. To complicate matters further, in Western academia, whereas Christianity was always taught by Christians, and Judaism was always taught by Jews, Islam was never allowed to be taught by practicing Muslims (who were considered too 'biased'). Thus in Western academia, Muslims read, studied and to a certain extent, believed, purportedly 'academically-objective' Orientalist works about Islam. Worse still, leading universities in the Islamic world—in awe of the West's superior science and technology—imitated the West in all spheres and thus taught and studied these same Orientalist works. This issue was—and is—not a peripheral one, but central to the very future of Islam because 80% of all Muslims in the world cannot speak or read Arabic, and because more Muslims speak English than Arabic.

The old days of Orientalism, thankfully, are now largely over, or should be—at least for Muslims. There have now, *wa'l-hamduLillah*, been three generations of Muslim scholars in the West gradually debunking all the Orientalist prejudices and contrived theories on Qur'an, Hadith and Islamic Law, in English. The 'first generation' were (and are—God preserve them!) scholars from the Islamic World—like Ismail Faruqi; Fazlur Rahman; Seyyed Hossein Nasr; Taha Jaber Alwani; Syed Naquib al-Attas and Akbar Ahmad—who successfully made the transition into Western academia (virtually or in person). The 'second generation' are mostly now middle-aged scholars and translators who are Western converts—like Hamza Yusuf Hanson; T.J. Winter (Abd al-Hakim Murad); Sherman Jackson; Nuh Ha Mim Keller; Ingrid Mattson and the prolific Aisha Bewley—who travelled to the Islamic world and spent years studying Arabic and Usul sciences and later translated, published and taught the gems of Islamic thought in English. The 'third generation' are powerful younger scholars like Jonathan Brown; Faraz Rabbani; Feras Hamza; Joseph Lumbard and Caner Dagli who are as comfortable in traditional Islamic scholarship as they are in Western academia. It is true that many Western universities are still teaching the books that are essentially Orientalist—or 'Orientalist-lite'—in outlook; and it is true that most major academic and commercial publishing houses will generally only print these kind of books—HarperCollins occasionally, and SUNY Press being notable exceptions—but it cannot be denied that the tide has turned in Islamic Studies, and that naked Orientalist prejudice has generally moved from universities to conservative 'think-tanks'. It is equally true that this has largely come about through the work of Western Muslim scholars, translators, preachers, social activists, N.G.O.s and above all, perhaps, independent publishing houses and websites. And it is even more remarkable that they have done this, over the last twenty-five years, against a historical and political background where the West has been drawn into more confrontation with the Islamic world than any time before for centuries, and where, tragically, there has arisen in the Islamic world new extremist fringe groups (albeit openly rejected by 99% of Muslims in the West and in the Islamic world, who tellingly make up 90% of their victims) as violent, intolerant and inhumane as many Western prejudices feared.

Howbeit, it is not without significance that this year, 2014 CE, marked the first awarding of accredited BA degrees by the US's first

Muslim Liberal Arts College, Zaytuna College (in Berkeley, California). Indeed, this event, though largely unnoticed by the world at large, can be taken to formally mark the beginning of the end of Orientalism in serious Islamic Studies in the West. And the fact that, despite being a predominantly Sunni College, they asked the great Islamic philosopher, Professor Seyyed Hossein Nasr to be their commencement speaker, is undoubtedly an extremely positive, and hopeful sign, *in sha Allah*.

To that end, I have prepared a list of 100 books covering the different aspects of Islamic Studies. Whatever its shortcomings, one thing it does not suffer from is the inclusion of any Orientalist writings. It is high time Messrs Rodwell, Goldziher, Margolioth, Noldeke, Guillaume, Rosenthal, Schacht, Gibb, Bell, Lewis, Cragg, Cook, Crone and company—*and their intellectual heirs*—are thanked warmly for their interest, and their books are transferred from the 'Islamic Studies' shelves in libraries to the 'historical fiction' shelves. And anyone purporting to write about Islam in the future must have more than a dictionary-aided knowledge of written Arabic, but must speak Arabic fluently, have studied *Usul* and know or have seriously tried to learn the Qur'an and significant sections of the Hadith *by heart*. This is the bar that Muslim scholars themselves have to meet, but to my knowledge there is not a single non-Muslim scholar who has ever learnt the Qur'an—let alone the Hadith—by heart. I believe most Islamic scholars would warmly welcome such a change, and indeed it has always shocked me how major professors and writers in the West, who teach and write on Islam, cannot speak or read Arabic properly and do not even know *Juzu' 'Amma* by heart. I venture to say, moreover, that some of the misunderstanding that politicians and the media labour under in the West——and consequently, their erroneous policies—towards Muslims and the Islamic world is connected to this lack of application amongst its leading scholars.

About the List

This list represents over thirty years of reading. I cannot pretend to have read all the relevant books in English—especially those published in the Indian subcontinent. Nor can I pretend to be free of my natural prejudices and preferences as a mainstream Orthodox Sunni Muslim. I have to admit also that some of the books included here, I read in the original Arabic or even in French, but I have tried to look at the English translations of these before recommending them. Though there are many other excellent books I could well have recommended, I refrained from doing so because I wanted to limit the number of books to 100: this represents four years reading at over two books a month (some of which are quite long), and that is enough for up to the BA, and possibly MA, level: in short, it is sufficient for anyone apart from the specialist scholar. Life is short; books are endless, and beyond books, as Ghazali reminds his elementary students in *Ayyuha al-Walad*, is the practice of Islam.

For this reason also I have tried to choose the books according to four criteria:

1. I have tried to choose the books that have been the most influential (in their original languages, and over time) on Muslims themselves. In this I have been greatly aided by Ali Gomaa's recently published *Al-Kutub al-Mukawwinah lil-Fikr al-Islami al-Sunni* (available at: rissc.jo) which 'ranks' the most influential books in Islam. I have not always adopted the 'view from the Azhar', but I only diverge from it where I believe I have strong reasons.

2. I have tried to choose the spiritually *most useful* books available, and I have tried to make this less subjective by relying on well-known authorities.

3. I have tried to make the selection complementary; that is, I have tried to make the books fill the gaps left by each other, so that the whole list leaves as little as possible of the broader issues uncovered.

4. I have staggered the list in three tiers of increasing difficulty and length: (i) 25 Essential Books on Islam in English, (ii) 50 Excellent Books on Islam in English and (iii) 25 Recommended Books on

Islam in English. Thus the first 25 books (which I have selected to be as short as possible) can be read at high school level; the second 50 can be read at BA level, and the last 25 at MA level (albeit these last 25 are not significantly more difficult than the previous 50—they generally just provide further material and different viewpoints). All titles are well within the intellectual grasp of an educated and thinking layperson, especially if he or she follows the progression in difficulty per subject.

I should also probably forewarn the reader of the following points:
- I have not attempted to discover the best, most easily available or cheapest editions of each book—I leave that to better bibliophiles than I.
- I have tried not to make judgements on translations—the Qur'an excepted—since I have generally only read one translation of a book recommended on the list.
- Perhaps this is just my own ignorance, but it seems to me that the one sphere which Muslims have yet to recapture—not merely from their own perspective, but from an integral Qur'anic perspective on the cycles of time—is history. Consequently, the list relies heavily on (the best of) non-Muslim writers on Islamic history.
- I have not included traditional Arabic works covering subjects like Arabic grammar or Qur'anic recitation: there seems little point in talking about the *Alfiyyah* (even if it were fully translated) or recommending (progressively): the *Tuhfat al-Atfal*; the *Jazariyyah*; the *Shatibiyyah* and the *Tayyibat al-Nashr*, if people do not know Arabic.
- I have recommended a number of traditional works of Islamic Mysticism. What I have not done is recommend any works by 'modern teachers' of the kind that frustratingly fill the shelves of any bookshop in the West, be it the '*Tariqah-without-Shari'ah*' variety, or the contemporary Western Sufi adepts, putting forth their rather sentimental feelings of mysticism. I know that Rumi

is now the most popular poet in the West, but as I understand it, nothing is more rigorous, disciplined or ascetic than traditional Islamic mysticism, nor more committed to the *Shari'ah*—Ghazali's *Ihya* alone suffices to make this point.

- I have not included any of the well-written, well-meaning and well-publicized recent books on Islam (like: *No god but God: The Origins, Evolution, and Future of Islam* by Reza Aslan) despite some of the good that they have done, because I have found too many intellectual errors and misunderstandings in them.

- I have brazenly suggested a few of my own works—it is my list, after all…

Finally, it remains to be said that this list will doubtless change, year by year, as more books are published or other books come to light; also, undoubtedly, others will perceive things that I do not, and make their own, better lists. This list is meant as a baseline, as of 2014-2015. The shortcomings of its details are my own—may God forgive them and me—but I believe the basic idea can be of tremendous value, *in sha Allah*.

It must nevertheless be admitted that a person could read and more or less understand all of these books and still remain intellectually illiterate, scientifically ignorant and physically vulnerable in the face of the modern world. Accordingly, I have also provided a list of 40 'General, Necessary' books (seven of them reference books) that I have read and found enormously profitable that I believe every Muslim—and indeed every layperson—would profit by reading. A Muslim does not have to know a lot about everything, but he or she should not be completely ignorant of the world around them either. God says in the Qur'an:

Say: 'Behold what is in the heavens and in the earth!' But signs and warners do not avail a folk who will not believe. (Yunus, 10:101)

And:

PART I

Have they not travelled in the land so that they may have hearts with which to comprehend, or ears with which to hear? Indeed it is not the eyes that turn blind, but it is the hearts that turn blind within the breasts. (Al-Hajj, 22:46)

And God knows best.

PART II
100 BOOKS ON ISLAM IN ENGLISH

25 ESSENTIAL BOOKS ON ISLAM IN ENGLISH
and
50 EXCELLENT BOOKS ON ISLAM IN ENGLISH
plus
25 RECOMMENDED BOOKS ON ISLAM IN ENGLISH

KEY:
25 ESSENTIAL BOOKS are in Arabic numerals
50 EXCELLENT BOOKS are in lower case Roman numerals
[SHORT READ]=Under 100 pages
[LONG READ]=Over 700 normal pages approx
[TCT]=Translation of a Classical Text

100 BOOKS ON ISLAM IN ENGLISH: 25 ESSENTIAL & 50 EXCELLENT BOOKS ON ISLAM IN ENGLISH

(A) Introductions to Islam

A) (I) General Introductions to Islam in English

1) *Understanding Islam and the Muslims* (T.J. Winter and John A. Williams/Fons Vitae, USA, 2003, 99pp)
—This is a very simple, pictorial, Q-and-A book on essential questions in a winning format. [SHORT READ]

2) *Ideals and Realities of Islam* (Seyyed Hossein Nasr/Islamic Texts Society, UK, Revised edition, 2001, 226pp)
—An excellent general introduction addressing both Sunni and Shi'i denominations of Islam.

3) *The Vision of Islam* (Sachiko Murato and William C. Chittick/I.B. Tauris, 2nd Revised edition, 2006, 408pp)
—The best teaching guide on Islam in English.

❧

i) *Islam: A Concise Introduction* (Huston Smith/HarperCollins, USA, 2001, 112pp).
—This is actually a chapter from the best-selling modern book on religion ever (2.5 million + sold), *The World's Religions* (2nd Edition), by Prof. Huston Smith. [SHORT READ]

ii) *What is Islam and Why?* (Ghazi bin Muhammad/Islamic Texts Society, UK, 2012, 53pp; also available online at www.freeislamiccalligraphy.com)
—An explanation of the meaning and relations between Islamic rites. [SHORT READ]

iii) *Understanding Islam* (Frithjof Schuon/World Wisdom Books, USA, New edition, 2004, 204pp)
—Islam from the point of view of 'Perennial Philosophy' by its foremost exponent, but contains metaphysical insights about Islam not to be found in any other book.

A) (II) Essentials of Islamic Religious Knowledge

4) *The Absolute Essentials of Islam* (Faraz Rabbani/White Thread Press, California, USA, 2nd edition, 2008, 49pp).
—An excellent summary of the essentials of Islamic knowledge from the point of view of the Hanafi School of jurisprudence. [SHORT READ]

5) *The Practical Guidebook of Essential Islamic Sciences*, From *Ibn Ashir's Al-Murshid Al-Mu'in* (Ibn Ashir, trans. Shaykh Ali Laraki Al-Husain/Meem Institute, UK, 2nd Revised edition, 2014, 191pp) [SHORT READ] [TCT]
—A translation of and commentary on *Ibn Ashir's Al-Murshid Al-Mu'in*, the classical short primer of essential Islamic knowledge in the Maliki School of jurisprudence. (The original Arabic is a poem).

6) *The Ultimate Conspectus* (Abu Shuja al-Asfahani, trans. Musa Furber/Islamosaic, USA, 2013, 182pp) [SHORT READ] [TCT]
—A translation of and commentary on '*Matn Abu Shuja*', the classical short primer of essential Islamic knowledge in the Shafi'i School of jurisprudence.

iv) *Maqasid: Nawawi's Manual of Islam* (Imam Nawawi, Nuh Keller

trans./Islamic Texts Society, UK, 2nd edition, 1996, 150pp) [TCT]
—A translation of and commentary on Nawawi's *Maqasid*, the classical medium-length summary of essential Islamic knowledge in the Shafi'i School of jurisprudence.

v) *Ascent to Felicity* (Abul Ikhlas al-Shrunbulali, trans. Faraz Khan/ White Thread Press, California, USA, 2010, 224pp) [TCT]
—A translation of and commentary on Shrunbulali's *Maraqi al-Sa'adat*, the classical medium-length summary of essential Islamic knowledge in the Hanafi School of jurisprudence.

(B) Qur'an, Tafsir and Qur'anic Sciences

B) (I) Qur'an and Tafsir

7) *The HarperCollins Study Qur'an* (S.H. Nasr editor/HarperCollins, USA/*Forthcoming 2015*) [LONG READ]
—An excellent forthcoming translation of the Qur'an and selected commentaries, which I was privileged to see in manuscript form.

N.B.: Other excellent translations of the Qur'an are those of Abdullah Yusuf Ali (the unrevised version); Mohammed Marmaduke Pickthall; M.A.S. Abdel Haleem and the RABIIT translation (available online at altafsir.com and greattafsirs.com). Of the other well-thought of translations: many Muslims like Muhammad Asad's translation, but I have found too many serious mistakes in it. Arberry's translation is very poetic—and one feels he really loved the Qur'an, uniquely so, perhaps, amongst the older Orientalists—but again there are a lot of clear errors. Laleh Bakhtiar's has the virtue of being internally co-ordinated so that words are consistently translated the same way and comes with a concordance. Finally, I found that Alan Jones's translation contained some deep misunderstandings.

8) *Tafsir Al-Jalalayn* (Jalal al-Din Suyuti and Jalal al-Din Mahalli, trans. Yousef Meri/Fons Vitae, USA, 2008, 701pp; also available

online for free at: altafsir.com; greattafsirs.com and rissc.jo) [TCT]
—An excellent translation of the most famous and popular classical short *Tafsir* of the Qur'an.

🌿

N.B.: Until RABIIT's Great Tafsirs Project (published in hardcopy by *Fons Vitae*, KY, USA), no complete translations of *Tafsirs* (interpretation and commentary) of the Qur'an existed in English except those of Mawdudi and Syed Qutb, and no complete translations of Classical *Tafsirs* existed at all in English (notwithstanding two doctored translations of Ibn Kathir). Probably the most influential three *Tafsirs* in history are Tabari's *Jami' al-Bayan* (which comprehensively gathers the transmitted material for the first three centuries of Islam), Zamakhshari's *Kashaf* (which is considered the supreme linguistic *tafsir*, despite the author being considered a Mu'tazili) and Razi's *Mafatih al-Ghayb* (considered to be the greatest 'theological' *Tafsir*). RABIIT has commissioned partial translations of both Razi and Tabari (the late Yahya Cooper started translating Tabari but did not get past the first thirty or so verses of the *Baqarah*). Fons Vitae is due to bring out the volume on Tabari soon, God willing.

All these (plus many more, and all the Arabic originals) are available online for free at the seminal website www.altafsir.com and its sister site for iPhone and iPad www.greattafsirs.com.

🌿

vi) *Tafsir Al-Qurtubi* vol. 1 (Imam Al-Qurtubi, trans. Aisha Bewley/ Dar Al-Taqwa, UK, 2009, 787pp) [TCT] [LONG READ]
—An excellent translation (abridged—but only as far as repetition and linguistic notes are concerned—not for polemic reasons)—of Qurtubi's great *Tafsir*. It includes the *Fatihah* and the *Baqarah*, and also the principles of *Tafsir*, which are invariably at the beginning of Classical Tafsirs.

vii) *Asbab Al-Nuzul* (Al-Wahidi, trans. Mokrane Guezzou/Fons Vitae, USA, 2010, 304pp; also available online for free at: altafsir.com;

greattafsirs.com and rissc.jo) [TCT]
—Wahidi's *Asbab al-Nuzul* (the 'circumstances and ostensive causes' of [particular] verses of the Revelation of the Qur'an) is the seminal work on the subject; later commentators have questioned certain details and added others, but it is nevertheless the basic reference work on the topic.

B) (II) Qur'anic Studies:

9) *The Jewels of the Qur'an* (Ghazali, trans. M. Abul Quasem, [or Laleh Bakhtiar]/Great Books of the Islamic World, USA, 2009, 206pp) [TCT]
—Ghazali's masterpiece on the different kinds of Qur'anic verses.

10) *A Treatise on the Heart (Bayan al-Farq bayn al-Sadr wa'l-Qalb wa'l-Fu'ad wa'l-Lubb)* (Al-Hakim Al-Tirmidhi, trans. N. Heer, in *Three Early Sufi Texts*/Fons Vitae, USA, 2003, 175pp) [TCT] [SHORT READ]
—Despite the title of the collection and of the text itself in English (*Three Early Sufi Texts*; 'A Treatise on the Heart') the text is more an application of Tirmidhi's exegetical principle of *mana' al-taraduf* ('no tautology in the Qur'an'—he has a longer book by that name precisely) and for that reason constitutes an essential and brilliant text of *tafsir bil tafsir* (interpreting the Qur'an by 'self-referentiality'). The two short Sulami texts also translated in this volume are very instructive as well.

viii) *Introduction to the Sciences of the Qur'an* (Ahmad Von Denffer/The Islamic Foundation, UK, 2nd edition, 1994, 200pp)
—A good general introduction to the sciences of the Qur'an and to the rules of Qur'anic interpretation.

ix) *The Perfect Guide to the Sciences of the Qur'an* (Jalal al-Din Suyuti, trans. Hamid Algar/Garnet, UK, 2012, 301pp) [TCT] [LONG READ]
—This is only volume 1 of 4 of Suyuti's *Al-Itqan fi 'Ulum al-Qur'an*

which is the apogee of the Qur'anic Sciences; further volumes are promised.

x) *Asbab al-Nuzul* (Al-Wahidi/Fons Vitae, USA, 2009, 304pp) [TCT]
—A translation of the seminal text on the historical context of Qur'anic verses.

xi) *The History of the Qur'anic Text* (M.M. Azami/UK Islamic Academy, 2003, 376pp)
—A crucial work to understand how the Qur'anic text has been preserved.

(C) Seerah, Sunnah and Hadith

C) (I) On the Seerah
(The life of the Prophet ﷺ)

11) *Muhammad: His Life Based on the Earliest Sources* (Martin Lings/Islamic Texts Society, UK, 2nd revised edition, 1983, 376pp)
—The definitive work on the life of the Prophet ﷺ in the English language.

C) (II) On the Sunnah
(The customs and actions of the Prophet ﷺ)

xii) *Riyad al-Saliheen* (Imam Nawawi, trans. Salah Al-Din Yusuf [or Aisha Bewley]/DarulSalaam, Pakistan, 1999, 1455pp) [TCT] [LONG READ]
—Nawawi's keystone work; essential for knowing the full gamut of the *Sunnah*.

C) (III) On the Hadith and its Sciences

12) *Forty Hadith* (Nawawi, trans. E. Ibrahim and Denys Johnson-Davies/Islamic Texts Society, UK, bilingual English-Arabic edition, 1997, 132pp) [TCT] [SHORT READ]

—Nawawi's beautiful selection of forty *Ahadith*, by way of introduction to Hadith in general.

13) *Forty Hadith Qudsi* (selected and trans. E. Ibrahim and Denys Johnson-Davies/Islamic Texts Society, UK, bilingual English-Arabic edition, 1997, 152pp) [TCT] [SHORT READ]
—A beautiful selection of forty *Ahadith qudsiyyah*—*Ahadith* wherein God Himself speaks through the Prophet ﷺ.

14) *Hadith: Muhammad's Legacy in the Medieval and Modern World* (Jonathon A.C. Brown/Oneworld, UK, 2009, 304pp)
—A recent well-rounded survey of the whole science.

xiii) *Sahih Muslim* (various translations, some available online for free) [TCT] [LONG READ]
—The shorter of the two most authentic and influential collections of the Prophet Muhammad's ﷺ sayings (later arranged by Nawawi).

xiv) *Sahih Bukhari* (various translations, some available online for free) [TCT] [LONG READ]
—The longer of the two most authentic and influential collections of the Prophet Muhammad's ﷺ sayings (later arranged by Nawawi).

xv) *Hadith Literature: Its Origin, Development & Special Features* (Muhammad Zubayr Siddiqi/Islamic Texts Society, UK, 1993, 192pp)
—An assessment of the science, particularly suited to responding to its Orientalist detractors.

xvi) *An Introduction to the Science of Hadith: Muqadimmat Ibn Al-Salah*, (Ibn Al-Salah al-Shahrazuni, trans. E. Dickson/Garnet, UK, 2006, 384pp) [TCT]
—A classical text explaining the science of *Hadith*.

N.B. Various other traditional collections of *Hadith* (namely: Tirmidhi; Ibn Hanbal; al-Nasa'i; al-Sijistani; al-Darimi and Ibn Maja), and the later canonical collections (such as those of Bayhaqi; Baghawi; Nawawi, and 'Asqalani) have also become available as well.

🌸

(D) Islamic Doctrine (*'Aqidah*), Theology (*Kalam*) and Philosophy

D) (I) Islamic Doctrine (*'Aqidah*)

15) *The Creed of Imam Al-Tahawi* (trans. Hamza Yusuf Hanson/Zaytuna, USA, 2008, 168pp) [TCT] [SHORT READ]
—Tahawi's creed is the most influential of all Sunni doctrinal creeds. It should have been translated two hundred years earlier.

16) *Doctrines of Shi'i Islam*, (Ja'far Sobhani, trans. by Reza Shah Kazemi/IB Tauris, UK, 2001, 160pp)
—An overview of fundamental Shi'ite beliefs from a leading contemporary Shi'i Ayatollah.

🌸

xvii) *Al-Ghazali's Moderation in Belief* (Ghazali, trans. Aladdin M. Yaqub/University of Chicago Press, USA, 2013, 336pp) [TCT]
—A translation of Ghazali's *Al-Iqtisad fil I'tiqad*, Ghazali's most influential work on Islamic *'Aqidah*.

xviii) *The Lives of Man* (Imam Haddad, trans. Mostafa Badawi/Fons Vitae, USA, new edition, Quilliam Press, UK, 2003, 100pp,) [TCT] [SHORT READ]
—Not 'doctrine' as commonly conceived, but a definitive Qur'anically-based exposition of the human condition and future and past lives.

xix; xx) *Kitab al-Tawhid* and *Asl al-Din al-Islami* [SHORT READ]

(Muhammad bin Abd al-Wahhab/various translations available online for free)
—These two tracts form the backbone of Wahhabi—and to a certain extent Salafi—doctrine, and as such are necessary to understand this ideology.

N.B. The *Asl al-Din al-Islami* is barely ten pages long, but is the basis of the modern practice of *takfir*. Note also: Muhammad bin Abd al-Wahhab (1703-1792 CE) was historically too recent and in methodology too much of a rupture with Classical tradition for these texts to be categorised 'Classical'.

D) (II) Theology

17) *Imam Abu Hanifa's Al-Fiqh al-Akbar Explained* (Imam Abu Hanifa, with Abul-Muntaha and Ali al-Qari's Commentaries, trans. Abdur Rahman ibn Yusuf/White Thread Press, UK, 2007, 240pp) [TCT]
—Abu Hanifa's theological treatise is probably the earliest and arguably the most influential theological treatise in Islam.

xxi) *Islamic Philosophy and Theology: An Extended Survey* (Montgomery Watt/Edinburgh University Press, UK, 1985, 184pp)
—An older, dated work by an Orientalist scholar (some of whose other works are problematic), but still useful for its comprehensiveness and academic equidistance.

D) (IIa) The Nahj al-Balagha

N.B. The *Nahj* is a unique collection of the sermons and letters of Ali bin Abi Taleb (k.w.). It is accepted by Shi'a scholars as authentic, and after the Qur'an and the four principle Shi'i collections of Hadith (Kulayni's *Kitab al-Kafi*; Ibn Babuya's *Man la Yahdarruhu al-Hadith*; and Mohammad al-Tusi's *Tahdhib al-Ahkam* and his *Al-Istibsar*), is the most important religious sourcebook for Shi'a Muslims. Its ideas touch on many topics including theology; spirituality; metaphysics; *fiqh*; *Tafsir*; Hadith; prophetology; ethics; social philosophy; history; politics; administration; civics; science; rhetoric; poetry; and literature. Most Sunnis have disputed its authenticity, but some have accepted it, and some have even written commentaries on it (including Razi, Taftazani, and, at the end of the nineteenth century, Mohammad Abduh).

xxii) *Nahj al-Balagha* (Ali bin Abi Talib [k.w.]; complied Sharif Radi, trans. Yasin al-Jibouri/Tahrike Tarsile Qur'an, Elmhurst NY, USA, 7th edition, 2009, 990pp). [TCT]
—A one volume translation of the *Nahj*.

D) (III) Philosophy

18) *A Young Muslim's Guide to the Modern World* (S.H. Nasr/Islamic Texts Society, UK, 1994, 280pp)
—An indispensable guide to the Islamic Weltanschauung (for Muslims of all ages).

19) *Ibn Tufayl's Hayy ibn Yaqzan* (Ibn Tufayl, trans. Lenn Evan Goodman [or Budd]/University of Chicago Press, USA, 2009, 280pp) [TCT]
—Ibn Tufayl's Andalusian classic not only reconciles reason, mystic knowledge and the Shari'ah, but summarizes Islamic philosophy and does it in a charming story.

☙

xxiii) *Islamic Philosophy from its Origin to the Present* (Seyyed Hossein Nasr/SUNY, USA, 2006, 380pp)
—Nasr does not simply go through who thought what (as did Majid Fakhri, with a certain academic disbelief, in his *A History of Islamic Philosophy*) but explains what the real issues are, and how they are resolved, as only someone who has actually understood them can do.

D) (IIIa) The Philosophy of Love in Islam

xxiv) *Love in the Holy Quran* (Ghazi bin Muhammad/Islamic Texts Society, UK, 7th expanded edition, 2014, 548pp)
—A systematic account of all the different kinds of love based strictly on the Qur'an, originally a PhD thesis at Al-Azhar University in Cairo, translated by Khaled Williams and the author himself.

xxv) *The Ring of the Dove: A Treatise on the Art and Practice of Arab love* (Ibn Hazm, trans. A.J. Arberry/Luzac Oriental/UK, 1996, 2008pp) [TCT]
—Another charming Andalusian classic but from the now-extinct *Dhahiri Madhhab*, this time on romantic love (mostly).

(E) Islamic Jurisprudence (*Usul Al-Fiqh*) and Law (*Shari'ah*)

E) (I) Islamic Legal History

xxvi) *A History of Islamic Legal Theories: An Introduction to Sunni Usul al-Fiqh* (Wael Hallaq/Cambridge University Press, UK, 1999, 306pp)
—A study of Islamic legal theory from its beginnings until the modern period.

E) (II) Islamic Jurisprudence (Usul Al-Fiqh)

20) *Al-Shafi'i's Risala* (Imam al-Shafi'i, trans. Majid Khadduri/Islamic Texts Society, UK, 1997, 380pp) [TCT]
—The *Risala* is the seminal, and most influential, text in *Usul*.

xxvii) *Principles of Islamic Jurisprudence* (Mohammad Hashim Kamali /Islamic Texts Society, UK, 2005, 550pp)
—A good outline of the principles of Islamic jurisprudence and their application.

xxviii) *Imam al-Shatibi's Theory of the Higher Objectives and Intents of Islamic Law* (Ahmad Al-Raysuni/IIIT, London; Washington D.C., 2005, 478pp)
—An introduction and analysis of Shatibi's important theory of *Maqasid al-Shari'ah*—to our knowledge the only one in English.

E) (III) Islamic Law (Shari'ah)

21) *Responding from the Tradition: One Hundred Fatwas by the Grand Mufti of Egypt* (Ali Gomaa, trans. T. Elgawahry and N. Freidlander/ Fons Vitae, KY, USA, 2011, 320pp)
—A hundred of the most frequently asked questions, convincingly and simply answered.

☙

xxix) *Al-Muwatta of Imam Malik ibn Anas*, (Imam Malik, trans. Aisha Bewley/Diwan Press, UK, 3rd edition, 2014, 766pp) [TCT] [LONG READ]
—The first and still-most-powerful manual of Islamic rulings on every conceivable issue at the time of Imam Malik by Imam Malik himself.

xxx) *The Reliance of the Traveller: 'Umdat al-Salik* (Ahmad ibn al-Naqib al-Misri, trans. Nuh Keller/Amana Publications, Bethesda, USA, revised edition, 1997, 1232pp) [TCT] [LONG READ]
—A classical manual on an array of legal rulings from the point of view of all four Sunni *Madhhabs*, carefully annotated by the translator.

xxxi) *War and Peace in Islam: The Uses and Abuses of Jihad* (Ed. Ghazi bin Muhammad, I. Kalim, M.H. Kamali/Islamic Texts Society, UK, 2013, 554pp)
—A comprehensive treatment of the subject of jihad by various leading scholars, including some important essays in translation and two excellent essays reproduced from Lumbard's *Islam, Fundamentalism and the Betrayal of Tradition*.

PART II

(F) Islamic Mysticism (Sufism) and Spirituality

F) (I) Introductions to Sufism

22) *What is Sufism?* (Martin Lings/Islamic Texts Society, UK, new edition, 1993, 134pp)
—An eloquent survey in English.

🌿

xxxii) *A Sufi Saint of the Twentieth Century* (Martin Lings/Islamic Texts Society, UK, 3rd edition, 1993, 242pp)
—Shows Sufism in practice, not merely in theory.

xxxiii) *Sufism* (William C. Chittick/Oneworld, UK, 2007, 224pp)
—Another excellent survey of the subject, but more academic.

F) (II) Classical Sufi Texts

N.B. Unlike almost any other dimension of Islam, Sufi texts have been extensively and well-translated into English for over a hundred years (notwithstanding poetry like that of Hafiz [in Persian] or Ibn al-Farid in Arabic which are practically impossible to translate). If we consider the most influential Sufi texts to be (1) Qushayri's *Risalah*; (2) Ghazali's *Ihya 'Ulum al-Din*; (3) Ibn 'Ata' Allah's *Hikam*; (4) Abu Talib Makki's *Qut al-Qulub*; (5) Ibn Al-Arabi's *Al-Futuhat al-Makkiyah*; (6) Ansari's *Manazil al-Sairin*, and (7) Rumi's *Mathnawi*—then we note that all of them have been translated (albeit the *Futuhat* only in part, because it is so long) except the *Qut al-Qulub* (which is also over 800 pages), in addition to dozens of other Classical Sufi texts. This is in stark contrast with *Tafsir* (as noted earlier); with Hadith collections (which are never translated by Westerners, but rather by Islamic institutes) or even Islamic theology (the works of Ash'ari and Razi for example have yet to be translated). This is no doubt because Sufism represented, to Western academics, 'Eastern Mysticism' without Shari'ah or Sunnah, or indeed, commitment, which is precisely the opposite of Classical Sufism.

23) *Mukhtasar Ihya 'Ulum al-Din* (Revival of Religious Sciences, abridged) (Imam Ghazali, trans. Marwan Khalaf/Spohr, Cyprus, 2013). [TCT]
—This is purportedly Ghazali's own abridgement of the *Ihya*; even shorter abridgements include Ghazali's *Alchemy of Happiness* (*Kimiya' al-Sa'adat*) and *Al-Arba'in fi Usul al-Din*. There are several translations of the *Alchemy of Happiness* available online for free and it is also a good start for beginners, if a shorter read is required. Many sections of the *Ihya* have been well-translated into English; see for example the ongoing translations of the *Ihya* by the Islamic Texts Society. The only complete one (by Kitab Bhavan, Delhi, 1982) requires considerable editing (and is very long, obviously).

xxxiv) *The Book of Wisdom* (Ibn 'Ata' Allah al-Iskandari, trans. Victor Danner/Paulist Press International, USA, new edition, 2002, 233pp). [TCT] [SHORT READ]
—This is an excellent scholarly translation of the *Hikam*; the volume also contains Abdullah al-Ansari's *Munajat*.

xxxv) *Stations of the Wayfarers* (*Manazil Al-Sairin*) (Abdullah al-Ansari, trans. Maryam al-Khalifa Sharief/Fons Vitae USA, 2000) [TCT]
—This edition also contains the Arabic text of Ansari's masterpiece *Manazil al-Sairin*; I have to say, it is not quite as well translated as Nahid Angha's *Stations of the Sufi Path*—which is Ansari's earlier, Persian version of the same basic text—but it is a good effort and contains the original Arabic, which is invaluable.

xxxvi) *Mathnævi* or *Masnævi* (Rumi, trans. Reynolds Nicholson [or Mojaddedi]/Gibb Memorial Trust, UK, 3 volumes, 2nd revised edition, 1982) [TCT]
—Rumi's poetic magnum opus.

xxxvii) *Speech of the Birds: Mantiq al-Tayr* (Farid ud-din Attar, trans. Peter Avery [or Darbandi or Harvey]/Islamic Texts Society, UK, 1998, 582pp) [TCT]
—A charming but powerful allegory of the mystic quest.

F) (III) On Ibn Al-Arabi

N.B. Though Ibn al-Arabi is considered by some Muslims to be heretical (or rather, consider the *Fusus al-Hikam* to be so), many Sufis consider him to be Islam's greatest mystic.

xxxviii) *The Sufi Path of Knowledge* (William Chittick/SUNY Publications, NY, 1989, 504pp)
—The most comprehensive examination of Ibn al-Arabi's teachings available in any European language.

xxxix) *The Quest for Red Sulphur* (Clause Addas/Islamic Texts Society, UK, 1993, 348pp)
—An excellent biography of the Andalusian Mystic.

F) (IV) Devotional Litanies

N.B. These usually consist of verses of the Qur'an; recitation of the Divine Names; *Ahadith*; supplications (*du'a*) from the Hadith and *tasbih* (glorification of God) and salutations on the Prophet ﷺ—sometimes constructed in poetic meter. They are used regularly by Muslims as supererogatory devotions (*nawafil*) especially by women during the times they cannot pray or touch the Qur'an.

24) *Dala'il Al-Khayrat: Original Arabic, Transliteration and Translation to English* (compiled: Ali Elsayed/Naqshbandi-Haqqani Sufi Order of America, 2011, 350pp) [TCT] [SHORT READ]
—A useful edition which makes it easy to read in transliteration for those who do not know Arabic.

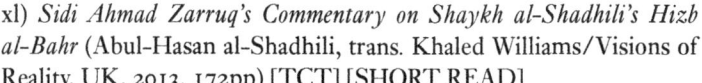

xl) *Sidi Ahmad Zarruq's Commentary on Shaykh al-Shadhili's Hizb al-Bahr* (Abul-Hasan al-Shadhili, trans. Khaled Williams/Visions of Reality, UK, 2013, 172pp) [TCT] [SHORT READ]
—*Hizb al-Bahr* is perhaps the most beloved influential litany recited

in the Islamic world after the *Dalail*. Sidi Ahmad Zarruq's commentary is widely considered to be the best explanation of it.

xli) *The Mantle Adorned: Imam Busiri's Burda* (Imam Busiri, trans. Abdal Hakim Murad/Quilliam Press, UK, 2009, 180pp) [TCT]
—A lovely translation with the Arabic original and a selection of helpful quotations.

F) (V) Spiritual Psychology

xlii) *Fragrant Knowledge of Thoughts* (Al-'Urf al-'Atir) (Al-'Eidroos, trans. Mokrane Guezzou/RUTAB/Jordan, forthcoming 2014) [TCT]
—A truly remarkable spiritual analysis of 'incoming thoughts' extensively read in the Ba 'Alawi faith movement.

(G) Other: History, Culture, Art; Science, Language, Dreams and Politics

History of Islam

25) *A History of Islamic Societies* (Ira Lapidus/CUP, UK, 3rd edition, 2014, 1304pp) [LONG READ]
—An excellent one-volume history of Islam.

☙

xliii) *The Venture of Islam* (Marshall Hodgson/University of Chicago Press, USA, 3 volumes, 1977)
—The standard academic history; excellent notwithstanding aspects of the early history.

xliv) *The Muqaddimah of Ibn Khaldun* (Ibn Khaldun/trans. Franz Rosenthal, Princeton University Press, Abridged edition, 2004, 512pp) [TCT] [LONG READ (in full)]
—A jewel of historiography, and actually of everything.

PART II

Culture

xlv) *Moorish Culture in Spain* (Titus Burckhardt/Fons Vitae, USA, 3rd edition, 2001, 227pp)
—A wonderful summary of the Andalusian period.

Art

xlvi) *The Art of Islam* (Titus Burckhardt/World Wisdom Books USA, Commemorative edition, 2009, 248pp)
—A beautifully-illustrated masterpiece on the subject.

Science

xlvii) *Islamic Science: An Illustrated Study* (Seyyed Hossein Nasr/Kazi Publications, 1976, 273pp)
—Another beautifully-illustrated masterpiece on its subject.

Language

xlviii) *Arabic through the Qur'an* (Alan Jones/Islamic Texts Society, UK, 2005, 348pp)
—For the non-Arabic-speaking Muslim, this book is an ideal introduction to the Arabic language, since all Muslims have to know a little Arabic for prayer.

Dreams (Oneiriology)

xlix) *Ibn Seerin's Dictionary of Dreams* (Al-Akili/Pearl Publishing House/Penn, USA, 1992, 512pp)
—Includes most, if not all, of Ibn Seerin's seminal text, but categorised under contents of the vision alphabetically; very useful in practice.

Politics

l) *Al-Ahkam al-Sultaniyyah: The Laws of Islamic Governance* (Abul

Hasan al-Mawardi, trans. Asadullah Yate/Ta Ha, UK, 1996, 400pp) [TCT]
—Mawardi's text is a dry read and does not seem very relevant to the present, but it is probably the most influential classical work on the legal duties and powers of rulers.

25 RECOMMENDED BOOKS ON ISLAM IN ENGLISH

Introductions to Islam

1. *Islam and the Destiny of Man* (Charles le Gai Eaton/Islamic Texts Society, UK, 1994, 262pp)
—A very well-written and engaging older Western introduction to Islam.

Quranic Studies

2. *An Anthology of Qur'anic Commentaries, Vol.1* (trans and ed. Feras Hamza, Sajjad Rizvi and Farhana Mayer/OUP in association with the Institute of Ismaili Studies, UK, 2008, 668pp) [LONG READ]
—A remarkable selected anthology, despite its representing the Ismaili engagement with the Qur'an as essentially textual.

3. *The Story of the Qur'an* (Ingrid Mattson/Wiley-Blackwell, UK, 2013, 312pp)
—An enjoyable but scholarly account of how the Qur'an has been studied generation after generation.

Islamic Jurisprudence

4. *The Four Imams and their Schools* (Gibril Haddad/Muslim Academic Trust, UK, 2007, 576pp)
—An intense look at the Imams of the four *Madhhabs*.

PART II

Islamic Mysticism

5. *Purification of the Heart* (Hamza Yusuf/Starlatch Press, USA, new revised 5th edition, 2012, 212pp)
—Hamza Yusuf Hanson's excellent translation and commentary on a nineteenth century spiritual text. This book has already done a lot of good. It is a support on the Sufi path based on the Qur'an, the Hadith and the *Ihya*.

6. *The Doctrine of the Sufis* (Kitab Al-Ta'arruf li Mathahib al-Tasawwuf) (Abu Bakr al-Kalabadhi, trans. A.J. Arberry/CUP, 1977, 173pp)
—An early but systematic explanation of the doctrine and practice of *Tasawwuf*.

7. *Sufis of Andalusia* (Ibn Arabi, trans. R.W.J. Austin/University of California Press, 1971)
—A short foretaste of Ibn Arabi's thought and milieu.

8. *Divine Love* (William Chittick/Yale, USA, 2013, 520pp)
—In my review of the book, I wrote: "Chittick is arguably the best scholar and translator of classical Islamic mysticism (Sufism) the Western world has ever produced. His books are sheer gold. But this latest work is a masterwork studded with unique spiritual gems on love."

9. *On Invoking the Divine Name* (translations from Ghazali and others/MABDA, Jordan, 2012, available online for free at: www.rissc.jo) [SHORT READ]
—A small but important collection of texts on the invocation of the Divine Name by Ghazali and others; subsumes most of the Hadiths cited by Suyuti's *The Remembrance of God* (Natijat al-Fikr fil-Jahr fil-Dhikr) which is also available online for free at: marifah.net.

Islamic Culture

10. *Fez: City of Islam* (Titus Burckhardt/Islamic Texts Society, UK, 1992, 176pp)

—A fascinating look not just at Fez, but Maghribi Islamic culture and history.

11. *Mecca, from Before Genesis until Now* (Martin Lings/Archetype 2002, 84pp) [SHORT READ]
—An excellent short introduction to the sacredness of Mecca.

Islamic Art

12. *Splendours of Qur'an Calligraphy and Illuminations* (Martin Lings/ Thames and Hudson Ltd, 2005, 454pp)
—The best explanation of the subject with some splendid illustrations.

Medicine

13. *Medicine of the Prophet* (Ibn Qayyim al-Jawziyya, trans. Penelope Johnstone/Islamic Texts Society, UK, 1998, 350pp) [TCT]
—The standard work on the subject, beautifully produced.

Science

14. *The History and Philosophy of Islamic Science* (Osman Bakar/ Islamic Texts Society, UK, 1999, 276pp)
—An intelligent overview of the topic.

15. *The Bible, the Quran and Science* (Maurice Bucaille/Islamic Book Service, New edition, 1999, 252pp)
—This book, by a famous convert to Islam, caused a sensation when it first came out and is probably still one of the best of its kind—trying to correlate Qur'anic verses and scientific facts—though obviously the venture is fraught with intellectual dangers as empirical science yields new findings, and as language is 'stretched' to try to accommodate these.

PART II

Islam and the West

16. *Islam and the West: The Making of an Image* (Norman Daniel/ Oneworld, Oxford, UK, 2009, 472pp)
—A seminal, eye-opening account of Christian views and prejudices about Islam over history.

History

(Some important vignettes of Islamic History, chosen from different periods and places)

17. *Saladin: The Triumph of the Sunni Revival* (Abdul Rahman Azzam/ Islamic Texts Society, UK, 2014, 282pp)
—Azzam's account of one of Islamic history's greatest heroes is not only the best of its kind, it is the only one that explains the role and influence of the *Nizami Madrassah* system on the Sunni Revival.

18. *The Crusades through Arab eyes* (Amin Maalouf/Saqi Books, UK, 1984, 312pp)
—An excellent summary of the time of the Crusades in general.

19. *The Graves of Tarim* (Engseng Ho/University of California Press, 2006, 388pp)
—The Yemeni da'wa was one of the most successful in history; this is an interesting 'anthropological' study of the subject.

20. *The Sabres of Paradise* (Leslie Blanch/Tauris Parke Paperbacks, new edition, 2004, 520p)
—An intriguing account of the epic of Imam Shamil and of the Daghestani resistance.

21. *My Life by Alhaji Sir Ahmadu Bello* (Ahmadu Bello/Cambridge University Press, 1962 reprinted thereafter, 246pp)
—This is an enjoyable autobiography of an intelligent and deeply pious Muslim—a descendant of Uthman Dan Fodio—who was the

first premier of the Northern Part of Nigeria, and one of its 'founding fathers'. It sheds light not only on the Muslim African experience, but also the Colonial and Post-colonial ages. It is also indispensable to understanding Nigeria itself.

22. *The Mantle of the Prophet* (Roy Mottahedeh/Oneworld, Oxford, UK, 2009, 384pp)
—A historical account of the Iranian Revolution interspersed with historical fiction, itself based on the experiences of a real Ayatollah; a masterpiece of writing and history.

23. *Ibn Battuta's Travels* (Ibn Battuta, ed. Tim Mackintosh-Smith/ Picador; new edition, 2003, 352pp) [TCT]
—Ibn Battuta's much-loved famous travels.

24. *The History of Al-Tabari* (39 volumes) (Muhammad ibn Jarir al-Tabari/State University of New York Press) [TCT] [LONG READ]
—Tabari's *magnum opus* on history, translated.

Language

25. *Lane's Arabic-English Lexicon* (Islamic Texts Society, UK, 1984) [LONG READ]
—Lane's completed dictionary remains the best Arabic-English dictionary on Classical Arabic.

PART III
33 GENERAL, NECESSARY BOOKS AND 7 REFERENCE WORKS

Religion

1. *The Bible* (New King James or New Jerusalem translations) [LONG READ]
—The Bible does not say what people think it does. It needs to be read for itself.

2. *The World's Religions* (Huston Smith) (2nd Edition)
—The best one-volume book on the subject, which goes to the heart of each of the religions.

3. *Tao Te Ching* (Lao Tze) [SHORT READ]
—This mysterious Taoist classic bears repeated contemplation.

4. *Black Elk Speaks* (John Neihardt)
—This moving work gives real insight into Native American religion and history.

History

5. *Histories* (Herodotus) [LONG READ]
—The first history book ever written; a splendid, sometimes fantastical, read.

6. *The History of the World* (J.M. Roberts) (3rd Edition) [LONG READ]

—The best one-volume summary of world history, notwithstanding a dubious rendering of the rise of early man.

7. *A History of Christianity* (Paul Johnson) [LONG READ]
—This is a good summary of Christian history, but there are others equally fine.

8. *The Rise and Fall of the Great Powers* (Paul Kennedy) [LONG READ]
—This book not only relates the last five hundred years of world history, but also crucially explains the necessary balance between military and economic might.

9. *The Prize* (Daniel Yergin) [LONG READ]
—This book retells the history of the Twentieth century through the lens of its most important commodity: oil.

10. *Wild Swans: Three Daughters of China* (Jung Chang) [LONG READ]
—This book retells the tragic history of Twentieth century China through personal narratives.

Philosophy

11. *The Complete Plato* [LONG READ]
—Alfred North Whitehead once described the whole of philosophy as a series of footnotes on Plato and Aristotle, and indeed there is hardly a philosophical issue that Plato does not inquire into. It is sometimes difficult for the modern reader to read the polytheistic Greek mythology in Plato—not to mention the homosexual pederasty that the Greeks seemed to practice (though he does not himself like it)—but nevertheless there are inimitable precious gems in Plato, and reading him is in itself an education. The best dialogues (in our humble opinion) are: *Meno*; *Crito*; *Phaedo*; *Phaedrus*; *The Symposium of Love*; *Timaeus* (though strange in parts); *The Sophist* and of course *The Republic*.

12. *The Complete Aristotle* [LONG READ]
—A lot of Aristotle's writings are dry and consist of (basically incor-

rect) ancient science, but some are intellectually indispensable, such as *De Anima*, the *Poetics*, and the *Organon* (his works on logic).

13. *The Consolations of Philosophy* (Boethius) [SHORT READ]
—A pleasant and completely convincing treatise on the virtues of philosophy.

14. *Commentary on Plato's 'Symposium' on Love* (Marsilio Ficino, trans. Sear Jayne)
—Arguably the best mortal work ever written on the science of love.

15. *The Pelican History of Western Philosophy* (D.W. Hamlyn)
—Bertrand Russel or Coppleston's histories of philosophy are usually recommended, but Hamlyn's is shorter and less polemical than either.

16. *The Crisis of the Modern World* (Rene Guenon) [SHORT READ]

17. *The Reign of Quantity and the Signs of the Times* (Rene Guenon)
—In these two works, Guenon explains the modern world in a way that no one else has, and even though these books are about a hundred years old, they are even truer today than when they were written.

18. *Logic and Transcendence* (Frithjof Schuon)
—This philosophical text provides an inoculation and antidote to the quagmires of twentieth century philosophy.

Law

19. *The Rule of Law* (Tom Bingham) [SHORT READ]
—This wise little book teaches volumes about government, justice and the law.

Science

20. *A Short History of Nearly Everything* (Bill Bryson)
—Arguably the best written one-volume history of science written; replaces Asimov's (now anyway outdated) *New Guide to Science* as a popular science primer.

Geography

21. *Guns, Germs and Steel* (Jared Diamond)
—An illuminating and seminal look at how geography influenced—if not determined—the course of human history.

Environment

22. *Collapse* (Jared Diamond)
—Diamond's other masterpiece; shows the effect of climate and the environment on human history *and on its future*.

Nature

23. *The Secret Lives of Dogs* (Elizabeth Marshall Thomas) [SHORT READ]
—This book seems an odd fit on a great works list, but contains a more sympathetic understanding of the society and emotions of animals than any other book.

24. *The Secret Life of Trees* (Colin Tudge)
—This book is a stunning description of the amazing functions and interactions of trees.

Health and Survival

25. *The Art of Chi Kung* (Wong Kiew Kit) [SHORT READ]

26. *The Complete Book of Tai Chi Chuan* (Wong Kiew Kit) [SHORT READ]
—Chi Kung and Tai Chi promote long term health, rather than merely treating illness (like modern medicine). These two books are the best guides to their practice.

27. *Convict Conditioning* (Paul "Coach" Wade)
—Everybody has a body; in addition to cardio-vascular fitness, bodies need strength. Despite the style and dramatic narrative of the book, it is the best available that shows how to build real strength

in the body, in a healthy way, without expending too much time and without ever needing a gym or equipment.

28. *The SAS Survival Handbook* (John "Lofty" Wiseman, Revised edition) [SHORT READ]
—A survival guide for emergencies and in nature is something that no person—no matter how or where they live—can reasonably neglect in their lives, and this book is considered one of the best.

Literature

29. *The Iliad* (Homer) (trans. Rieu, Lattimore or Fagles)
—*The Iliad* is the first epic ever written. When presented with a priceless casket and asked what to keep in it, Alexander the Great said 'a copy of *The Iliad*'. Because of its beautiful 'parataxis' style, and because of Achilles's dramatic movement from passion to compassion, it was considered by the ancient Greeks as the finest poetry ever. It is also one of the most culturally influential books ever written.

30. *The Odyssey* (Homer) (trans. Rieu, Lattimore or Fagles)
—The word '*nostoi*' ('return') in Ancient Greek is related to the word '*nous*' meaning 'intellect'. The epic poem of Odysseus's return home is thus not merely a great story but a symbolic tale representing the return of the intelligence to the Spirit—and it was taken by ancient Greeks like Porphyry to mean precisely that. *The Odyssey* is arguably even more culturally influential than *The Iliad*.

31. *Three Theban Plays* (Sophocles) (trans. Fagles and Knox,) [SHORT READ]
—The ancient Greeks themselves—for whom tragic drama had a sacred, cathartic function—considered Sophocles (with Aeschylus) the best playwright ever, and his Theban Plays are considered the best dramas ever composed because they most perfectly show the clash between human will and inexorable destiny.

32. *Don Quixote* (Cervantes, trans. Edith Grossman or Cohen) [LONG READ]
—Don Quixote is not only the first novel and the funniest novel ever, it is arguably the last novel possible (intellectually, not chronologically—novels have obviously not stopped since) for it summarizes all the romances and epics before and shows (and that is its stated purpose) how they warp a reader's mind so that in the end he confuses fiction with fact. It is even also the start of meta-fiction. At any rate we hold it to be the best novel ever, as did one hundred of the world's top authors in 54 countries in 2012.

33. *The Complete Shakespeare* [LONG READ]
—Not all of Shakespeare's plays or sonnets need to be read, but some of his sonnets are arguably the best in the English language, and his plays are not only the best since Sophocles for the language, but also for their human content. In particular we recommend *Hamlet* for his dramatic movement, and his coming to be 'ready' for action, and for death; *King Lear* for his learning humility through his own folly; *Macbeth* for its portrayal of evil and its futility; *Othello* for its symbolic portrayal of the Fall (Othello being the soul, Desdemona, the Spirit and Iago representing the Devil) and *Romeo and Juliet* for its timeless portrayal of romantic love.

7 Reference Works (in their latest editions)

N.B. These books are necessary reference works. Few people read them systematically but in the case of the *Mayo Clinic Family Health Book*, it is very readable.

1 *Mayo Clinic Family Health Book*

2 *The Oxford English Dictionary*

3 *Roget's Thesaurus*

4 *The Times Atlas of the World*

5 *Grey's Anatomy*

PART III

6   *The Cambridge Encyclopedia*

7   *The CIA World FactBook (despite the publisher's other activities)*

About the Author

HRH Prince Ghazi bin Muhammad bin Talal (b. 1966) was educated at Harrow School; received his BA in Comparative Literature from Princeton University in 1988 *Summa cum laude*; his first PhD (in Modern and Medieval Languages and Literatures) from Trinity College, Cambridge University, UK, in 1993, and his second PhD (in Islamic Philosophy) from Al-Azhar University in Cairo in 2010. He is a Professor of Philosophy at Jordan University and Chief Advisor to HM King Abdullah II for Religious and Cultural Affairs.